T0072506

Embracing Healing

A Slow Down Thirty Day Practice

Christina Murphy, CHC, AADP

BALBOA
PRESS

A DIVISION OF HAY HOUSE

Balboa Press books may be ordered through booksellers or by contacting:

Balboa Press
A Division of Hay House
1663 Liberty Drive
Bloomington, IN 47403
www.balboapress.com
1 (877) 407-4847

Because of the dynamic nature of the Internet, any web addresses or links contained in this book may have changed since publication and may no longer be valid. The views expressed in this work are solely those of the author and do not necessarily reflect the views of the publisher, and the publisher hereby disclaims any responsibility for them.

The author of this book does not dispense medical advice or prescribe the use of any technique as a form of treatment for physical, emotional, or medical problems without the advice of a physician, either directly or indirectly. The intent of the author is only to offer information of a general nature to help you in your quest for emotional and spiritual well-being. In the event you use any of the information in this book for yourself, which is your constitutional right, the author and the publisher assume no responsibility for your actions.

Any people depicted in stock imagery provided by Thinkstock are models, and such images are being used for illustrative purposes only. Certain stock imagery © Thinkstock.

Print information available on the last page.

ISBN: 978-1-5043-4861-4 (sc)
ISBN: 978-1-5043-4862-1 (e)

Balboa Press rev. date: 01/18/2016

Dedication:

For those lost to us and those we love in the Lyme Community. Thank you to those who have helped me along the way in my journey.

Preface:

The practice of slowing down became very important to me when I became chronically ill. I had to take a look at the dizzying speed in which the world worked and re adjust because I just couldn't keep up.

I wrote a journal at this time. During this time a whole new world opened up to me. I began entering into chaos with a calm I did not know I had. On the days when I could not meet with my own expectations, let alone move, I read a few of my days' thoughts and it really helped me.

I am writing this book for all of us with illnesses, (and anyone else), so we can adjust to a happy place where we can be whole with who we are now.

We are all amazing at whatever velocity we fill our lives with.

Introduction:

The practice of slowing down is a very important part of healing. When someone is chronically ill it takes a while to accept circumstances and move into a healing plan.

This is also the case of people who are dealing with stress which can lead to illness.

This book is designed to help the healing process. It is a thirty-day adventure with a mandala and saying to meditate or think on as coloring each day.

By focusing on one saying for five minutes or more each day one can slow down and feel better about choices for the day.

In this manner calm and new discoveries about yourself will occur.

Do one per day and enjoy.

Day 1

Slow Down; The skies are still above and the ground is still beneath you. You are NOT responsible for everything, just you and just now.

Thought to think on: Just be for a moment. Breathe. What one thing is most important to do today? If you get that done, celebrate because you are awesome!

Day 2

Remember a happy time, a lovely friend or a moment that brings a smile to your face.

Taking a few moments to remember good things brings serotonin into the brain. It gives a sense of wellbeing and exercises your memory. How wonderful to breathe for five minutes and be happy in it.

Day 3:

Think of one blessing you have and celebrate that. Good events are wonderful examples of how we will things to be. Owning it and breathing it equals creating it.

This is very important and as the days go by, more blessings will occur. Claim them, be one with them. Breathe deeply and think on them with your eyes closed. Each one evicts negativity from your mind and soul. Fill your thoughts and heart with positivity.

Day 4

Try not to think on your words and responses when you speak to someone. If you listen, truly listen, thoughts will spring up all on their own.

How many times have you felt, "no one is listening"! Take a deep breath and just actively listen during your next conversation. You will hear inflections and movement and see a whole new depth to the person speaking. It will improve your communication skills tenfold. New thoughts will come to your mind that may surprise and delight you.

Day 5

How extraordinary the patterns of the moon and sun as they rise and set. Admire them and see how they take their time to follow the paths before them.

It took me time to figure this out. Now my favorite vacation past time is to watch the sun set or the moon rise. They are never in a hurry and all of nature is affected by the course they take. Who am I to question taking my time so that something higher than myself can direct my path?

Sit, relax let the Sun and Moon show you how the road less traveled can be.

Day 6

Take nothing for granted. The quiet and smell of snow falling, the way the grasses move as they are touched by wind, how leaves dance when they fall on an Autumn day and how the yard smells after a summer rain.

During the winter, the news casts can heighten our fears of not getting things done, but sitting on a porch and watching the snow fall, when no one is around, has a sound of its own and it is very calming. So is stopping to watch and listen to the common everyday things we do not always observe.

Peace and comfort can be found in daily happenings.

Day 7

What a joy to look at your food and enjoy every bite of it. It tantalizes the senses with smell and texture. What a blessing!

Closing our eyes and smelling our food and slowly enjoying how it looks and feels gives a sense of wellbeing as it nourishes our body. Can we honestly say that "fast" food helps us to digest and give our bodies the time it needs to replenish the fuel it has lost? Permit yourself to enjoy to savor and to recharge while feeding yourself.

Day 8

When gifted with knowledge either learned or by a natural knowing or possession, do not bend it by force or plan or scheme. Be thankful for it and see what doors of opportunity will open for you. Your purpose will become clear as it arrives naturally.

How many times have we planned to do one thing or another and a few other things pop up and we turn away from it because we didn't "plan on that"? Stop for a few minutes, breathe deep and recall instances that repeated where you did work that brought you joy. Perhaps that is where your path lies.

Day 9

Take time to play. Every now and then, (if you have children), talk with them, play and see how fun it is. Even big kids can play now and then. It brings out the joy and relaxed person you can be.

When we get bogged down with life and all of its circumstances, we forget to play. We forget to enjoy ourselves or "Snoopy dance". Take a few minutes to play or do something that makes you giggle. It's good for you. Treat the little kid in you.

Day 10

Invite quiet in your life by establishing places at work and home where reflection and peaceful thoughts can flourish. You earned it.

Sometimes all it takes is a tiny space where you can take a breath or think on good thoughts to recharge those batteries. You are worthy of those precious moments. Honor yourself with a 5-minute refresher.

Day 11

Admit it! We all need a day to be lazy. Rest is very important for the body. It is necessary.

Many of us burn our candles at both ends and then wonder why we are so tired. Resting is not only important but is warranted for a healthy body.

Day 12

Close your eyes. Listen to voices on the wind. It is timeless. Feel it.

There are moments when hearing the sounds of a child laughing, a dog barking, a radio playing and in my neighborhood, bag pipes playing is priceless. These sounds carry in the air and make our now amazing.

Day 13

Partition your Big jobs into smaller jobs. It has taken over 40 years for the internet to get to where it is. Something to ponder!

I always seem to make either a huge list or a giant project for myself. If I can accomplish one tiny thing a day, I am grateful. Soon enough, everything will fall in place as if I did that big job easily. Thank heaven for loving myself. By doing all the small things with ease, we can show the big finale with grace and fluidity.

Day 14

All the achievements you have done in your life are fantastic! Think on them from time to time to bring you comfort.

Everything that we do has an impact on our environment and community. Think of the amazing contributions you have made, from a smile to cheer up a child to a program that was put into use in a big company. One word or action can be the lift you need to cheer up your day. (As well as someone else's!)

Day 15

Talk slower or don't talk. The measure of communication is by both listening and by words.

    Giving someone the space to say all that they wish with a true effort to listen is a gift. The words we say can also be a gift. Take time and just be in the moment for a conversation.

Day 16

Consent to be late at times. A strict itinerary is not an act of living. Life is. It just is. Be and breathe.

Having deadlines and have to's is very stressful and stress kills or at minimum creates an opening to ill health. Relax. The sky will still be there, the world still spins. Breathe in, breathe out.

Accept what is and live.

Day 17

Listen to the song of a bird. The complete song. Music and nature are Gifts.

When I worked at a museum, one day I laid in the grass like I was going to make a snow angel and just let the apple blossoms fall and truly listened to the birds. It changed me. I felt an energy and rejuvenation I cannot begin to express. Try it sometime, even if you just put your feet in the grass and listen. It is amazing.

Day 18:

Stand back! Let others be leaders and take their turn at opportunities. There will be future projects and circumstances where you can be in front again.

This I think is a hard one for me and I still try hard to let go. By standing back though I have learned how other people handle things and how even though we all do things differently it's all good! I learn. As long as I learn I am living life! All good!

Day 19:

Taking action is good and necessary, but taking time to think is awesome. Taking the time to ruminate, consider and reflect can be rewarding.

Have you ever rushed and did a project and stepped back and take a look at it? I wish I had a few times. Being successful is not just in action but taking the time to think and look at all the possibilities.

Day 20:

Do the things YOU like to do. Your inner child needs recreation and release. Make time for play! Age? Who cares!

  Go to a movie, play cards or play a video game. Want to go hiking or canoeing? Go! Color in coloring books, just do it! Whatever pleases your inner child, do it!

Day 21:

Observe the night sky and the stars. It whispers to you.

Take a blanket and watch the sky. There is something larger than ourselves and lets us know we are but an inkling in infinite space. I feel less hurried and peaceful looking at the stars.

Day 22:

When you speak, listen very carefully to your words. When you pray, listen to your words, especially in prayer.

Words contain energy as well as meaning. Be careful how they are used.

Day 23:

If you are walking somewhere, look up and give someone a smile. If you are in a line, offer a kind word. Open a door for someone when entering a building. Do one small kindness.

A smile, a nice gesture or a small pleasantry in the day can be uplifting. It is rare these days and should become a new trend. Doing these things can make one feel awesome.

Day 24:

Stop rushing! Why are you rushing and being anxious? Stop, think and learn. Maybe you will understand you better!

Why are we so eager to rush around and please others? What is it that we need to please ourselves? Learning about ourselves can be fascinating.

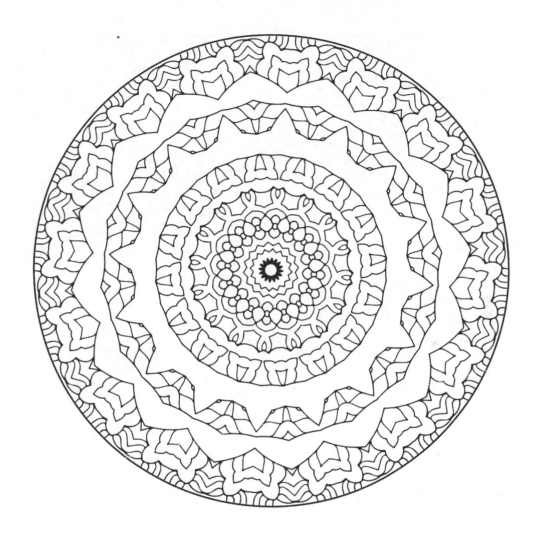

Day 25:

Want a smile or comfort and know you are giving to another? Pet a furry friend!

Four legged creatures are amazing for giving comfort and letting you give to them. If you can do more than five minutes of petting an animal, go for it. I have been known to rub my dogs' tummy often.

Day 26:

Walk for the sake of walking, not because you have to go somewhere.
Taking a walkabout is wonderful for seeing new things and to wander just to enjoy the sites.

Day 27:

Reading, whether it is poetry, a big book or an article, thoughtful reading is good for the soul.

There are just moments when I like to read a book or a good article. It helps me focus and gets me thinking about things. Reading is good.

Day 28:

Make something. Work with your hands. It gives your mind a vacation.

Whether doing a craft, building or cooking, making something keeps hands busy and the results are very gratifying.

Day 29:

Take a day to yourself. Being by yourself gives you great learning opportunities without becoming a monk or a hermit.

Sometimes going off on your own for a day or a weekend can give you a fresh perspective on things in your life and you don't have to leave your world behind.

Day 30:

When things are in a frenzied state and chaos, ask yourself; "what is <u>right</u> about this moment?" The probability is that you know what is wrong.

There are times when the choices we make can cause mayhem with our lives. Rethinking a circumstance and taking it easier sometimes produces a better result.

Bonus Healing thought:

Take time to wonder, to count blessings, to lift your face to the wind and let it cool your face or to enjoy the sunshine. A two-minute wonder can change an entire day.

This last one I try to do every day. When I find I am getting grumpy, I stop and take a breath or wonder how blessed I am to have a home and so many other things. I also do close my eyes and lift my head to the sunshine now and again. It fills me with comfort. When I go to the beach, I look down in the sand and wiggle my toes like I did when I was 5. All these things Help me relax and give me ease. I hope they will for you too.

About the Author:

Christina Murphy is a thriving Lyme patient, Mother, Grandmother, wife and Mom of a Redbone Coonhound named Rex. She has taken all she learned during her journey through Lyme and created a business to educate others about Lyme disease. She is a Wellness Coach that lives in Maryland and offers coaching for individuals and groups. She also educates at events.

She is twice certified by Institute of Integrative Nutrition and Affiniton/ Elymenate and is a proud member of the Frederick County Chamber of Commerce

Can Do with Lyme LLC
Candowithlyme2@gmail.com
Candowithlyme.com
301-473-2821

Printed in the United States
By Bookmasters